Introduction
The Passage of Time

How do we measure time? This may seem like a straightforward question with an obvious answer. But concepts of time are more than just the units of minutes, hours, days, and years. In a place like the abbey, and Glastonbury as a whole, the idea of time takes on new meaning.

Looking at the ruins, some of which date back over a thousand years, and trying to wrap our minds around the number of things they have borne witness to, is almost like trying to picture infinity. In the timeline of a place like this, we are the tiniest blip, and in the history of the planet, the events of this place are an even smaller blip.

We also consider time in different ways. We have the archaeological record, which today, due to advances in science like radiocarbon dating, we can date with relative accuracy. And then there is mythic time, within which the legends of the abbey exist. The stories woven about this place stand almost apart from time, in an age too distant to picture, and too remote to solidly grasp, but ever present.

Then there is everyday time, which some say moves differently here. Most residents of the town will know about 'Glastonbury Time', in other words, things happening 'in their own good time'. If you're a fan of schedules and strict punctuality, you might have to be prepared to let go of those ideals when you get to town! Taking some 'me time' to meditate under a tree in the abbey, you might find hours have slipped away. Or on rare occasion, perhaps you've been transported to another time altogether!

As we get older, time seems to pass by more quickly, due perhaps to the relative length of our lives. But we begin to appreciate time well spent, and our place in the history of things. For those of us fortunate enough to play a part in the history of the abbey, we can feel close to all those who have come before, at once distant in a linear sense but only a veil's breadth away from us.

The way that most of us observe time is in the turning of the year; through its seasons, and its festivals, both cultural and religious. Read on to see how some of these weave through a year in the life of Glastonbury Abbey...

January
What's a Wassail?

Every January, Glastonbury Abbey welcomes members of the community to the annual Wassailing of the orchard, to invite a fruitful year for our apple trees. But from where does the tradition stem? Wassailing is a tradition that may be older than the abbey itself. The word 'Wassail' derives from an Anglo-Saxon greeting that vaguely corresponds to "Good health". Imagine the scene, an Anglo-Saxon longhall, a roaring fire, and a bowl containing warm cider, mead or ale passed around to share and toast with. The lord proclaimed "waes hael!" to which came the reply "drink hael!" (drink well) and merriment would no doubt ensue.

This tradition of good cheer continued into the Middle Ages. In some parts of the country, wassailing involved groups of people going door-to-door requesting charity from the rich on Twelfth Night (January 5th). Songs would be sung, and pranks might be played if the householder didn't "bring us some figgy pudding", as the song goes, which may well be where our traditions of Christmas carolling and trick-or-treating come from. However, in the cider-making counties of the West Country, it is all to do with the blessing of the orchard.

5 Jan - Twelfth Night

West Country wassailers observe 'Old Twelfth Night' according to the old Julian calendar on January 17th (or in our case the nearest weekend to it) throughout Somerset. Glastonbury's event is led by the local branch of OBOD (Order of Bards, Ovates and Druids). Traditional songs are sung, noise is made to wake up the slumbering trees and ward off negativity, and the trees are toasted (quite literally, with pieces of toast as well as liquid libation).

The apples that abound in the area also find their way into Glastonbury legend. 'The Isle of Avalon' was equated by Geoffrey of Monmouth with 'Ynys Avallach' – meaning Isle of Apples. There is also a Somerset folk tale of the 'Apple Tree Man', the spirit of the oldest tree in the orchard. It is said if you please him, he will reveal the location of hidden gold. Whilst sadly there isn't any gold to be found in the ruins, the liquid gold of our Glastonbury Abbey cider and mead can be found year-round in our shop!

February
Signs of Spring

How do you mark the changing of the seasons? In the new year, everyone is eager for the coming of spring, and we look for little signs in nature. At the abbey, this is indicated by the first snowdrops, determinedly pressing their way up through the cold ground to decorate the ruins with their white flowers. If it has been a particularly mild winter, we might also see swathes of daffodils starting to sprout early, ahead of the day of their Welsh patron, St. David, on 1st March.

However, the start of February is the time of St. Brigid. Her feast day falls on the 1st and is now a public holiday in her native Ireland. It also corresponds with the Celtic seasonal festival of Imbolc and the Christian day of Candlemas a day later on 2nd February. The emphasis of both traditions is the returning light, and as we look around us at closing time at the abbey, day by day it gets just a tiny bit lighter, feeding our hope in anticipation of longer summer evenings.

Both Imbolc and Candlemas also have elements of ritual purification. Candlemas celebrates the presentation of Jesus at the Temple, and the Purification of the Virgin Mary, his mother. Imbolc, an Old Irish poem suggests, is marked by ritually "washing the hands, the feet, the head".

1 Feb - Imbolc, St. Brigid's Day
2 Feb - Candlemas

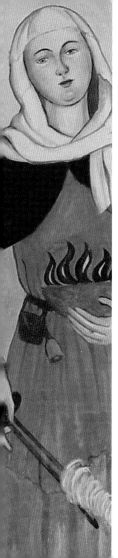

Some believe the name Imbolc to be Old Irish for 'in the belly' referring to the time prior to animals giving birth. It is a time of sowing seeds and spring cleaning of the house. Specific Irish traditions at this time include the making of a Brigid's Cross from rushes, making up a bed for St. Brigid who is said to pass by overnight, and leaving out strips of cloth for the saint to bless.

Many of the characteristics of the Irish goddess Brigid match those of the saint and are thought to have inspired Imbolc traditions. It was said to be the time when the hag of winter, the Cailleach, released her grip on the land and Brigid, representing the spring, returned. Hence why some believe the saint's day was chosen to fall at this time.

St. Brigid is said to have visited Glastonbury Abbey, following in the footsteps of St. Patrick. But unlike many of the saints, the abbey never claimed she was buried here, the monks only claimed the relics of some of her belongings. On the wall of St Patrick's Chapel you can see St. Brigid in a 2009 mural in the medieval style, holding a distaff and a flame, and accompanied by her cow.

The Spiritual Meaning of St Patrick's Day

One of the most celebrated saints' days is that of Saint Patrick, on 17th March. The larger-than-life revelry of Saint Patrick's feast day is reflected by the larger-than-life legends that surround him.

Despite being patron saint of Ireland, Patrick was born in Roman Britain (possibly even Somerset), captured by Irish raiders and taken to Ireland as a slave until his escape six years later. It is said he found his faith during captivity and as an adult returned to Ireland as a missionary.

One well known legend of Patrick is that he was said to have driven out all snakes from Ireland. Some see the snakes as an allegory for the pagans, with Patrick driving out old beliefs. Much more likely is it that a blend of the Celtic religion and the new Christian one was achieved; the saints stepping into the shoes of the druids. The astute Patrick would have recognised the value of this synthesis of religions and used recognisable symbolism to convey the message of the Christian faith. Four leaf clovers are usually synonymous with the luck of the Irish, but it is in fact the three-leafed clover, the shamrock, that is associated with St Patrick. He is said to have used its leaves to describe the Holy Trinity of Father, Son

1 Mar - St. David's Day
17 Mar - St. Patrick's Day
20 Mar - Spring Equinox

and Holy Spirit.

The annals of William of Malmesbury, chronicler to the abbey, say that Patrick came to Glastonbury and discovered its Old Church and twelve hermits living in cells surrounding it. The legend goes that they persuaded him to stay and become its first abbot, where he died and was buried. This is unsurprisingly contradicted by Irish sources which lay claim to Patrick's remains. Whether or not the saint did come to Glastonbury, Patrick's memory remained, one of the foremost amongst the lists of saints, and remembered in the name of St Patrick's Chapel.

The 17th of March is about more than shamrock hats, alcohol, and parades. It is a day when people of Irish ancestry, particularly in the USA, remember their roots across the miles. For many, Ireland is their spiritual home. We hope that for many of our members and visitors, Glastonbury Abbey is their spiritual home. Whilst many live locally, we have members from as far afield as Ireland and the USA. We hope for those of you that do not get to visit as often as you like, you are able to keep a feeling of connection to the abbey.

The celebration of Easter occurs in either March or April. It is quite literally a moveable feast! In some years Easter can fall almost a month later than the spring equinox, but the two are interrelated and often coincide. They also share some symbolism, as well as having accumulated some folkloric and secular elements over the centuries.

The vernal (spring) equinox is a fixed point in the solar cycle when days and nights are of equal length whilst the date of Easter is determined by a lunar calendar interacting with this date. Christian tradition holds that the Easter story occurred during the Jewish observance of Passover so aligns with this holiday. The date of Passover is the first full moon (the Paschal Moon) after the spring equinox (20th-21st March). To make things more complicated, there are two dates on which Easter is celebrated. The Western Church calculates this using the Gregorian calendar whilst Eastern Orthodox churches use the Julian calendar.

One Eastern Orthodox tradition relates to our modern Easter eggs. Boiled eggs are dyed red to represent the blood of Christ which, when cracked, represent his empty tomb. Legend tells

how Mary Magdalene went to spread the gospel at the court of the Roman Emperor and used the egg as a symbol of resurrection. When the Emperor replied that Christ's ascension was no more possible than the egg in her hand turning red, it promptly did so. Eggs were symbolic of rebirth and the new life that the season brings long before the advent of Christianity, so were an easily adopted symbol.

Easter and the equinox also represent a time of stillness before the launch into spring. During Holy Week, the week leading up to Easter, Catholics cover their altars and religious images with a cloth. This veil provides a pause, an intake of breath, in anticipation of the Easter celebration. For non-Catholics, this point of balance between winter and summer also provides a moment to pause and take stock. What has our time in the dark half of the year taught us? What fruits can be brought into being for the year ahead? If you have been dwelling on thoughts of a new project or a new beginning, now is the time!

May
Beltane Awakening

With a drum beat and a yell, the month of May begins with a call of 'wake up!'. The festival of May Day is halfway between the spring equinox and summer solstice, marking the time when summer really begins to emerge. Trees start to come into leaf, flowers bloom, and animals welcome their young. May Day is ushered in, up and down the country, with celebrations that include Morris dancing, May pole dancing, and the crowning of a young girl as May Queen. These customs have a strong fertility theme and basis in pre-Christian traditions. Since at least the 18th century, the Catholic Church has celebrated May as the month of the Virgin Mary and crowns statues of her with flowers as the Queen of May. This often involves young girls decorating Mary with flowers of hawthorn.

Until modern times, hawthorn trees were commonly decorated with ribbons after Easter as a 'May Bush'. The Glastonbury Thorn, or 'Holy Thorn', is a species of hawthorn, *Crataegus monogyna Biflora*. It is special not only because it flowers at this time of year and at Christmas, but because of its legendary origins. According to popular legend, the current Holy Thorns are descendants of the staff of Joseph

1 May - Beltane, May Day
19 May - St. Dunstan's Day

of Arimathea, which miraculously came into bloom when he planted it in the soil of Glastonbury. It is said to be of the same kind of thorn as that used for Christ's crown of thorns.

1st May is also celebrated as Beltane, with similar customs to May Day, and since it is one of four annual Celtic fire festivals (Beltane itself meaning 'bright fire'), bonfires are also lit, and small fires are leapt over for luck. In recent years, Beltane celebrations have become a big community event in Glastonbury, regularly attracting large crowds and photographers from the national press.

Celebrations normally begin and end within the grounds of the abbey near the Abbot's Kitchen, with a procession that winds its way through the town to congregate at Bushy Coombe on the slopes of Glastonbury Tor and back again. Foremost amongst the parade are the totems of the red and white dragons. These fiery beasts perhaps take on a more watery quality here and represent the red and white springs that flow from inside Glastonbury Tor. Others say they represent energy lines in the earth or the forces of winter and summer that do battle at this time of year, the white dragon of winter chased off into his lair for the next 6 months.

∽∾ June ∾∽
Glastonbury Tor Calling You Home

Despite the great height of its remaining ruins, Glastonbury Abbey is quite well hidden in the geography of the town, nestled at almost the lowest part of the landscape. Glastonbury Tor on the other hand stands prominent from miles around, a beacon that draws people to Glastonbury to come and explore. Besides a certain pop festival, many people flock to Glastonbury in June to celebrate the Summer Solstice on top of the Tor at the dawn of 21st June.

For many, when visiting Glastonbury or coming back to it from elsewhere, the first sight of the Tor is the signal of 'home'. It stands, 158m above sea level, an anomaly in the largely flat Somerset Levels. Topped by the remaining tower of the medieval church of St Michael, it is one of a number of high places in the southwest dedicated to the archangel.

The relationship between the Tor, visible from the abbey grounds, and the abbey is not well understood. Archaeological digs have shown occupation from at least the Post-Roman period of the 6th century, but it is not known if this was a monastic or purely secular settlement. A monastic presence is confirmed from at least the 13th century. Their relationship to the monks of the abbey is

20-21 June - Summer Solstice

not known, whether they were an offshoot or their own small community. However, it is likely that spiritual pilgrims would also have paid a visit to the Tor after visiting the abbey precinct, much as they do today. The Tor features prominently in several pieces of medieval Arthurian legend, and draws those seeking the entrance to the Underworld, or the secret resting place of King Arthur.

Both medieval and modern Glastonbury are known as places of pilgrimage and there is no better symbol of this than the Tor. The labyrinthine pattern of its slopes mimics the shape of a labyrinth like we see in churches and churchyards like St. John's, Glastonbury, and theories abound as to the origin of its contours, ranging from design by Neolithic settlers to being prescribed by leylines running through it. An ancient symbol, labyrinths in medieval times were used as a meditative 'micro-pilgrimage', a journey to the sacred centre in miniature, for those unable to travel long distances. Today the Tor stands over us and reminds us of all of our spiritual journeys, whether we choose to take the long winding path or the direct one to the summit.

July
A Pilgrim Revival

Pilgrimage is having something of a renaissance. When we think of the word, we often bring to mind devout medieval wanderers (or less than devout in the case of some of Chaucer's pilgrims of The Canterbury Tales). At Glastonbury, medieval pilgrims were drawn to see the site of the first Christian church in England and encounter the legends of King Arthur and Joseph of Arimathea.

The Reformation put paid to a lot of pilgrim activity in this country, but over the last century we have seen an increase in the popularity of pilgrimages. At Glastonbury, this included the start of annual Catholic and Anglican pilgrimages to the abbey which happen every July, and other forms of organised group and personal pilgrimages by those keen to follow in the footsteps of their medieval forebears. This was made literally possible when the Lady Chapel was renovated in 2014 and a medieval route was restored that took visitors past a holy well into the crypt of St Joseph.

Not just the abbey, but Glastonbury as a whole has become a place of pilgrimage for spiritual seekers of all backgrounds, and with its array of legends and sacred spots (which can be found on the town's pilgrim route, The Glastonbury Way),

2nd weekend in July -
Pilgrimage weekend

there is something for everybody.

Pilgrimages centre around sacred destinations but many pilgrims will tell you it is the journey that is the important part. This can involve time taken away from 'the real world'; time to work through your thoughts, get closer to the Divine, or just enjoy being in the Great Outdoors! Of course, with modern travel, many pilgrimages are no longer on foot. Those who cannot make such a journey will sometimes find mini-pilgrimages in the landscape that help replicate that meditative state such as labyrinths, like the one in the courtyard of St John's Church, Glastonbury. Others may even make virtual pilgrimages using the wonders of technology to try and experience something of the holiest sites in the world.

But why the increase in the 21st century of interest in pilgrimage? It may be a consequence of modern society that more people are finding themselves 'seeking' something. In Christian Europe of the Middle Ages, one of the reasons was the feeling of loss of Jerusalem, Christianity's spiritual centre. In the modern age it may be something less definable, a longing for a deeper connection in an ever-changing world. We hope that whatever the case, pilgrims to Glastonbury Abbey find a sense of peace and acceptance, and leave feeling fulfilled.

August
The Two Marys

Although monasteries like Glastonbury Abbey are thought of as male spaces, there is also a distinct air of the Feminine here. The abbey's Lady Chapel was the focal point of pilgrimage and was of course dedicated to the Virgin Mary. Today, people still come to this place to seek the Mother of God and many also seek the other Mary, the Magdalene.

Although there is little in the medieval chronicles of the abbey to indicate a visit by Mary Magdalene, she is remembered variously in the vicinity, in the Magdalene almshouses and the very street the abbey is on, Magdalene Street. She can also be found amongst the figures in the mural in St. Patrick's Chapel which replicates medieval church decoration. Here she is shown having the seven sins cast out of her as mentioned in the Bible. Today, many spiritual seekers, particularly women's groups, have reclaimed Mary Magdalene and see her as the first apostle, the semi-divine other half of Jesus Christ, and even mother of his child. Like Joseph of Arimathea and the abbey itself, Mary Magdalene is bound up with the story of what happened after the Crucifixion, and some believe she was amongst his companions when he first set foot in Avalon.

15 Aug - The Assumption of the
Blessed Virgin Mary

The height of summer is peak time for those seeking the two Marys. The feast day of Mary Magdalene falls upon 22nd July, whilst the Virgin Mary is honoured as Our Lady of Glastonbury a couple of weeks earlier at the annual pilgrimages, and more widely at the date of her bodily assumption into heaven on 15th August.

The Virgin Mary has been honoured here, some say, since the very beginning, some chronicles even claiming that Jesus dedicated the Old Church, the first on English soil, to her himself. In this church, it is said, was a statue of the Virgin Mary, the only object to survive the fire that destroyed the church in 1184. This wonderous statue was put on display in the newly erected Lady Chapel, built on the foundations of the Old Church, and was said to miraculously move during the singing of the Ave Maria.

Although the statue of Our Lady of Glastonbury did not survive the Middle Ages, its likeness may have been preserved in a medieval seal of the abbey, which in turn inspired the form of the modern Our Lady, which stands in the Church of St. Mary, opposite the abbey. And despite little of the Lady Chapel interior remaining, spiritually-inclined visitors often speak of the powerful but gentle energy this hallowed spot still holds to this day.

 September Spiritual Harvest

As summer starts to wane and we transition once more into autumn, the noticeable change in the season brings various things to mind; not just colder mornings, but spiritual observations too. September into October is the period of harvest for most of the northern hemisphere, and in many cultures, the agricultural calendar is tied to people's spiritual and religious beliefs.

In ancient times, a good harvest or a poor harvest could indicate the favour of the gods, or lack of, brought about by the actions of the community. The well-known phrase related to this, "we reap what we sow" indicates that what we send out into the world comes back to us. This applies not only to the proportion of effort we put into something in order to reap the rewards, but how we treat others and wish to be treated by them.

The law of reciprocity, or karma, in the Eastern religions, states that if we are kind to others, we are likely to receive kindness in return. Inversely, if we foster negativity, we risk attracting it back to us. This holds true in Christian teaching too.

22-23 Sep - Autumn Equinox

As Jesus said, "judge not, lest ye be judged", urging us to think before condemning others, when God may find we do not live up to such standards ourselves.

Harvest Festivals are celebrated in both the Anglican and Catholic calendars in Britain as early as 1st August — Lammas (from the Anglo-Saxon loaf-mass) which corresponds to the Gaelic Lughnasadh — and continue right through to the autumn equinox and end of September. Harvest festivals draw on ancient traditions and commonly will feature the presentation of a bread loaf made from the first wheat of the crop as a thanks to God for a bountiful harvest and are followed by a feast. Here in Somerset and the rest of the southwest, Harvest Home traditions continue to this day.

We may also think about the harvest in terms of spiritual sustenance. What is it that sustains us? What bolsters our reserves in preparation for the dark half of the year?

October
If Trees Could Talk

The coming of autumn is most noticeable in the changing colours of the trees. The abbey has many fine trees within its precinct and to some people who visit, these silent sentinels are of more interest than the ruins themselves. People take delight in being with trees; in greeting them like an old friend each time they pass by, in sensing their connection with the earth, and in watching them change as they cycle through the seasons.

If these trees could talk, what stories could they tell? Some of the oldest surviving trees onsite feature in historic photographs, such as the Holm Oak, thought to be 260 years old, visible in pictures of Bligh Bond's archaeological excavations in the early 20th century. And the Cedar on the lawn of Abbey House, probably planted when the house was built in the 1820s, that watched over generations of families that lived there.

Then there is the Yew, possibly the oldest tree in the grounds, and our most famous tree, the Holy Thorn, said to be a descendant of the original thorn that bloomed on Wearyall Hill from the staff of Joseph of Arimathea.

31 Oct - All Hallows Eve

Although trees may not physically speak, they can talk to us in other ways, with dendrochronology telling us what the climate was like centuries ago. Photos of tree-felling at the abbey in the first half of the 20th century show some trees with massive circumference that would have had hundreds of rings to examine.

Some are not quite so old but no less majestic. The Lime avenue which runs along the north edge of the church is younger, planted around 100 years ago, and whilst there wouldn't have been trees in this spot during the abbey's heyday, these gentle giants serve to remind us of the towering height of the buildings that have since disappeared.

Some trees are associated with special people. The Magnolia near the North Wall was the favourite tree of famous local author Geoffrey Ashe and was adopted in his honour for many years; now dedicated to his memory.

As temperatures start to drop, there is still delight to be found, crunching through the crisply textured orange- and yellow-toned leaves that coat the abbey grounds.

 November
All Saints and All Souls

All Saints Day (1st November) and All Souls Day (2nd November) are Catholic holidays to remember the dead. All Saints, also known as All Hallows, focuses on those who are in heaven. All of the saints, famous or obscure, right down to Christian family ancestors are prayed for.

All Souls is a day to pray for those in purgatory. In Catholic Latin America it is known as Day of the Dead, a much less sombre affair, more a colourful celebration of life. In many countries, on All Souls, bread and cakes are made and left on the graves of loved ones. In the Church of England, the day is called The Commemoration of the Faithful Departed.

In the 7th century, All Saints was originally held on 13th May, which coincided with Lemuria, a Roman sort of Halloween, and it's speculated to be why they chose that date. By the 9th century it had moved to 1st November in parts of Europe and by the 12th century the new date had taken over completely.

Glastonbury Abbey was a Benedictine monastery, and here The Order of Saint Benedict would have celebrated All Saints a full 6 months after the original date, on 13th

1 Nov - All Saints Day
2 Nov - All Souls Day
11 Nov - Rememberence Day

November. However, it was a Benedictine, Odilo of Cluny, who standardised the date of All Souls to be the day after the more widely celebrated All Saints Day of 1st November.

Early November in the Celtic calendar is Samhain. Irish tradition says it is a time when the veils between worlds are thin, and supernatural beings and souls of the dead cross over from the Otherworld to walk among us, an obvious influence on modern secular Halloween (All Hallows Eve) customs. Samhain was also a time of taking stock of the herds and slaughtering in preparation for winter. In Ireland, this tradition crossed over to St Martin's Day, 11th November, a celebratory feast day marking the end of the agricultural year and also coincides with Remembrance Day.

All Saints remained in the Protestant calendar after the Reformation, which also happens to be remembered on 31st October, or rather the act that is said to have sparked it. The date is not coincidental. On this day in 1517, Martin Luther chose to post his theses against the sale of indulgences on the door of All Saints Church, Wittenberg, Germany as he knew the church would be filled the following day with people coming to view the relics of the saints. Veneration of these relics would reduce the amount of time spent in purgatory, which was also the promise of those selling indulgences.

At this time of year many people of many faiths remember their ancestors and family members who have passed away, and in some traditions the whole month of November is given over to this process. So whatever your background, this November, spare a thought for those who have come before us, to whom we owe our being, and for the wisdom they hand down.

December
The Benefits of Darkness

At this time of year, many of us moan about the growing shortness of the days and getting up and going home in the dark (as well as getting to spend less time in the abbey grounds!). But we often miss the value that darkness has.

Western society is very focused on binary opposites: night and day, dark and light, and since the time of Scripture, 'dark' has been cast as evil or the absence of good (or God), equated with emptiness and the wilderness. The association may go back even further, to a time when humans developed a primal fear of the dark because of predators roaming at night.

However, without dark, how are we able to appreciate the light? If it was always summer, would you appreciate it?

Darkness has its own value too, beginning with the darkness of the womb in which we first develop. Sleeping in the dark is also best for our health. Animals appreciate the dark too, as it disturbs their rhythms when there is too much light pollution around.

Darkness is also a common aid for meditation and inner journeying. Guided visualisations often use the imagery

21 Dec - Winter Solstice
25 Dec - Christmas Day

or going down into the earth to symbolise going within ourselves to seek that which is hidden from our conscious minds.

Darkness is a form of sensory deprivation and if harnessed correctly can reduce stress, and aid self-healing and understanding. It helps to liberate us from physical attachments and all the stimulation of the physical world.

Finally, darkness is transformative. Like the earth and its animals waking up from hibernation, we emerge from the dark time of the year refreshed and ready for the first signs of spring.